THE

RECONSTRUCTION OF THE GOVERNMENT

OF THE

United States of America:

A DEMOCRATIC EMPIRE ADVOCATED,

AND

AN IMPERIAL CONSTITUTION PROPOSED.

BY

WM. B. WEDGWOOD, LL.D.,

Professor of Commercial, International, Constitutional, and Statutory Law, in the University of the City of New-York.

New-York:

JOHN H. TINGLEY, 152½ FULTON STREET.

1861.

RECONSTRUCTION OF THE GOVERNMENT.

UNIVERSITY OF THE CITY OF NEW-YORK,
August 23, 1861.

FELLOW-CITIZENS OF THE LATE UNITED, NOW BELLIGERENT STATES OF AMERICA:

To you who still hold sacred the declaration of the renowned statesman Henry Clay, and *even now* "Know no North, no South, no East, no West," but one great and glorious empire, bound together by ten thousand bonds of consanguinity and affinity—of time-honored duties performed and obligations gratefully acknowledged — of love and affection long cherished—of mutual pecuniary interests—to you would I present the strongest assurances of continued good-will and undiminished friendship. I would invite you to sit down with me and let us institute the inquiry, and ascertain if a reconstruction of our government can not be accomplished which will be satisfactory to all.

We are in the midst of extraordinary events. Civil war with all its horrors is upon us. Five hundred thousand American citizens are rushing to the battle-field, where father will be arrayed against the son, and brother against brother, in cruel and deadly strife. It will cost the nation in expenses for the war and in the destruction of private and public property more than five hundred millions of dollars for the first year with no certainty of seeing the end of the war at the expiration of the year. Is it not well for the whole nation, North and South, to pause and reflect before they plunge deeper into the yawning chasm before them?

Let us for a moment return to the old paths in which our fathers trod, and see if we can find any precedent to guide us in the dark hour that is upon us. Let us review the toil and suffering and sacrifice of our noble ancestors in constructing this republic, before we ruthlessly destroy it.

Before the Revolution there was no bond of union between the Colonies. When the battles of Lexington and Bunker Hill were fought in April and June, 1775, no one dreamed of establishing an independent nation. But, on Friday, June 7, 1776, the question of separation from the mother country was brought before the Continental Congress. The next day it was debated in committee of the whole, in secret session, and adopted. On Monday following, a committee was appointed to prepare Articles of Confederation. On the 4th of July, the Declaration of Independence was made public, and on the 12th of July the committee appointed to prepare Articles of Confederation made their report. But eighty copies of the report were printed; members binding themselves, their secretary, and their printer, by a solemn pledge of secresy.

The 8th of June, 1776, may be regarded as the birthday of this republic. On that day the umbilical cord which bound us to the mother country was forever severed. The infant republic was soon after to receive its baptism of fire and blood. New-York was to be the place forever consecrated by that august ceremony. The American army, under command of General Washington, was at that time in and around this city. In a few weeks thirty-five thousand of the best troops in Europe were at our doors. On the 27th August a desperate battle was fought on Long Island, a few miles from this city, in which more than a thousand brave American soldiers were killed, and still more wounded. On the following night the American army returned to this city, and a few days later Fort Washington, on Washington Heights, in this city, fell into the hands of the enemy, after a desperate resistance, and after the discharge of the last round of ammunition. Two thousand of the American army were here taken prisoners, and many slain. This was the baptism of the infant republic.

And who, I ask, were these illustrious men who were killed and wounded and taken prisoners, to suffer cruelties worse than death? The chivalric sons of the South stood side by side with the gallant sons of the North. They fought for the same cause. They shed their blood in defense of the same soil. Their last dying prayers were uttered for their country, and their whole country one and inseparable. Thus that holy band of revolutionary martyrs, from the sunny South and the frigid North fought and bled side by side in every battle of the Revolution from Lexington to Yorktown.

The Articles of Confederation were not adopted until nearly a year and a half after they were reported by the committee. The committee reported twenty articles; only thirteen were finally adopted. This was but little more than a union of sovereign States in a firm league of friendship with each other for their common defense, binding themselves to assist each other to resist all force offered against either of the States. The powers of Congress were such only as were necessary in carrying on the war, and then it amounted to little more than power to recommend, advise, and entreat. Under the Articles of Confederation the Revolutionary War was prosecuted and terminated, and our independence achieved.

Eight years of desolating war had made almost every house in the land a house of mourning. Fathers, husbands, brothers, sons, were missed from the family circle. The illustrious Commander-in-chief disbanded the remnant of his victorious army, imploring upon them ample justice from their grateful country, and the choicest blessings of heaven from the God of battles. As the veteran soldier laid aside his arms and returned to the home of other days, neglected and deserted, he keenly felt the fearful price which had been paid for liberty. To the one hundred and thirty millions expended, and the debt of fifty millions incurred, was to be added individual ruin, personal suffering, and loss of life.

On the 4th of December, 1783, the officers of the army assembled at Francis' Tavern in Broad street, in this city, for a final parting with their beloved Commander-in-chief. On entering the room where they were assembled, Washington said: "With a heart full of love and gratitude I now take leave of you. I most devoutly wish that your latter days may be as prosperous and happy as your former ones have been glorious and honorable." Each officer approached the chief, and Washington, incapable of utterance, bade each a silent farewell. Every eye was filled with tears and not one word interrupted the eloquent silence. They followed their chief to Whitehall in mute and solemn procession, where he entered a barge, and turning to his officers who stood uncovered upon the shore, and waving his hat bade them a silent adieu.

Immediately after the close of the Revolution the Confederated Congress recommended taxation and duties, but it had no power to levy and collect taxes or enforce the payment of duties. The Articles of Confederation were insufficient as a system of government. There was no longer the pressure of common danger which had given strength to the bonds of the Federal Union. The minds of the wisest and best men of the nation were filled with gloomy forebodings. They felt that there was an impending crisis in the affairs of the nation.

In 1784 Washington wrote: "The disinclination of the individual States to yield competent power to Congress for the Federal Government—their unreasonable jealousies of that body and of one another—and the disposition which seems to pervade each, of being all-wise and all-powerful within itself, will, if there be not a change in the system, be our downfall as a nation. I think we have opposed Great Britain, and have arrived at the present state of peace and independence to but very little purpose, IF WE CAN NOT CONQUER OUR OWN PREJUDICES." There was a general conviction in the public mind that some step must be taken to avert the impending calamity which hung over the country.

At length a gleam of light broke through the darkness. Virginia proposed a Convention of the Confederated States to consider and adopt some uniform system of trade and commerce for all the States. Five States met in Convention. They drew up a report recommending another Convention "to take into consideration the situation of the United States, and to devise such provisions as should seem to them necessary to render the Constitution of the Federal Government adequate to the exigencies of the Union."

Delegates were soon after appointed from all the States except Rhode-Island. The delegates, fifty-five in number, met and framed "The Constitution of the United States." They closed their sitting and adjourned. The members returned to their several States to advocate the approval and adoption of the Constitution they had framed. The following year, which is known as the year of suspense, at length drew to a close. The ratification of nine States was to be sufficient for the establishment of the Constitution between the States so ratifying the same. Before the 1st of July, 1788, Delaware, Pennsylvania, New-Jersey, Georgia, Connecticut, Massachusets, Maryland, South-Carolina, New-Hampshire, and Virginia, in the order here named, had approved and adopted the proposed Constitution. The event was every where hailed by the people with enthusiastic delight. Long processions, with banners and devices, and martial music, and ringing of bells, and firing of cannons, paraded the streets. Cities and villages were illuminated, and bonfires blazed on every hilltop in the country. Ten of the columns which were to support the federal edifice had been erected. The others were nearly completed. During the month of July the Constitution was accepted and adopted by the State of New-York.

As soon as nine States had accepted and adopted the Constitution, the Confederated Congress, then in session in the city of New-York, passed an act for the election of President, Vice-President, and members of Congress, under the new Constitution. The election was held. The new Congress met in the city of New-York on the 4th of March, 1789. On the 6th of April, a quorum being present, the ballots for President were examined and counted. George Washington was found to be unanimously elected. He was informed of his election. He proceeded at once to the city of New-York. All along the route he was greeted with irrepressible enthusiasm. All ages and sexes and conditions rushed forth to meet him. Triumphal arches were erected, and his pathway strewn with flowers. He was every where greeted with the roar of cannon, the sound of martial music, with songs and shouts of welcome.

At length the day arrived—the 30th of April, 1789—when Washington was to be inaugurated the first Chief Magistrate of this united and consolidated Republic. At nine o'clock the people assembled in their churches to implore the divine blessing upon the President and the Nation. At twelve o'clock Washington appeared on the colonnade of the City Hall, at the corner of Nassau and Wall streets, attended by his Cabinet and both Houses of Congress. In the presence of the hundred thousand freemen who thronged Wall, Nassau, and Broad streets, Chancellor Livingston read to the President the following oath:

"You do solemnly swear that you will faithfully execute the office of President of the United States, and will, to the best of your ability, PRESERVE, PROTECT, and DEFEND the CONSTITUTION OF THE UNITED STATES."

Washington pronounced the words of the oath clearly and distinctly after the Chancellor, and closing his eyes, with his whole soul absorbed in the supplication, he added, "So help me God!" and kissed the Bible lying before him. Chancellor Livingston then said to the multitude: "*It is done. Long live George Washington, President of the United States!*" Then was uttered such a shout of united and consolidated freemen as was never before heard on earth. The nation from that day entered upon the path of prosperity, greatness, and happiness, without a parallel in the history of the race.

The idea of a special Providence controlling, and aiding, and cherishing this nation, had long pervaded the mind of Washington and other leading minds in this country. At the close of the Revolution, when Washington had taken leave of the army, and appeared before the Confederated Congress to return his commission, he closed his memorable address to that body by saying: "I consider it an indispensable duty to close this, my last act of official life, by commending the interests of our dearest country to the protection of Almighty God, and those who have the superintendence of those interests to his holy keeping. Having now finished the work assigned me, I retire from the theatre of action, and bidding an affectionate farewell to this august body, under whose orders I have so long acted, I here offer my commission and take my leave of all the employments of public life." The reply on the part of Congress was as follows: "We join with you in commending the interests of our country to Almighty God, beseeching him to dispose the hearts and minds of its citizens to improve the opportunity afforded them of becoming a happy and respectable nation. And for you we address to him our warmest prayers that a life so beloved may be fostered with all his care, that your days may be as happy as they have been illustrious, and that he will finally give you that reward which this world can not bestow."

After Washington had taken the Presidential oath of office, he returned to the Senate Chamber in the City Hall, and in the presence of his Cabinet and both Houses of Congress, he delivered his inaugural address. In the course of this address he said: "It would be peculiarly improper to omit in this my first official act, my fervent supplication to the Almighty Being *who presides in the councils of nations*, WHO RULES OVER THE UNION, and whose providential aid can supply every human defect, *that his benediction may consecrate to the liberties and happiness of the people of the United States*, A GOVERNMENT INSTITUTED BY THEMSELVES FOR THEIR ESSENTIAL PURPOSES.

"In tendering this homage to the great Author of every public and private good, I assure myself that it expresses your sentiments not less than my own, nor those of our fellow-citizens at large less than either. *No people can be bound to acknowledge and adore the invisible Hand which conducts the affairs of men, more than the people of the United States.* Every step by which they have advanced to the character of an independent nation seems to have been distinguished by some token of providential agency; and in the revolution just accomplished in the system of this united government, the tranquil deliberations and voluntary consent of so many distinct communities, from which the event has resulted, can not be compared with the means by which most governments have been established without some return of pious gratitude, with an humble anticipation of the future blessings which the past seems to presage."

Admitting that God is the Supreme Legislator, and Ruler, and Judge—that his law is above all human compacts and constitutions and laws—that he presides in the councils of nations and controls the affairs of men, that he judges the world in righteousness and the people with his truth—let us compare his special providence in the affairs of our nation with the most signally favored nation of other days.

The descendants of the Patriarchs were in bondage in Egypt for four hundred and thirty years. Then God brought them out of Egypt, leading them by a pillar of cloud by day, and a pillar of fire by night. He opened the gates of the sea for their passage. For them rivers of water gushed from the flinty rock, and manna descended from heaven. He gave them his covenant amid the thunders of Sinai. For forty years he led them through the wilderness, until a new generation had been raised up and prepared for his service. He then drove out the heathen from Palestine, and there planted his chosen people, in thirteen States. The Ark of the Covenant was borne in triumph into the midst of that land. Prosperity and happiness followed them, and their name and their fame went out to the ends of the earth.

In the midst of their prosperity there was a dissolution of their Union. Eleven of the stars of the new constellation went out in darkness. The others were dragged from their orbit, and to this day are but wandering stars.

In after days God brought to the knowledge of the civilized world a new continent. He selected another people and planted them in the new world, in thirteen States. He drove out the heathen before them, and gave them the land for a perpetual inheritance. He led them through the Red Sea of the Revolution, and caused them at last to say: "The Lord has triumphed gloriously. The horse and the rider hath he thrown into the sea. Had not the Lord been on our side when the enemy came against us, we had fallen, we had perished."

He gave this people another covenant, by the hand of another Moses. Hundreds of thousands have regarded it as the gift of Divine Inspiration. The new covenant is still enshrined in the great heart of the nation.

For three-score years he has constantly extended our borders and strengthened the bonds which so long and so happily united us together. He gave us the lands of other nations, and as soon as they were ours, he revealed to us treasures of untold wealth, concealed from the beginning of the world. The flag of the thirteen stripes and ever-multiplying stars, was borne along the pathway of the nation, and the wilderness and the solitary place has blossomed as the rose. Industry, morality, religion, wealth, happiness, all the institutions of civilized life, have sprung up in our pathway at every advancing footstep. God has not dealt thus with any other nation. Surely the Lord of hosts has been with us. The God of Jacob is still our refuge. This God is our God forever and ever. He will still be our guide through this impending crisis, and if his will is consulted and followed, the world will say: "Blessed is that nation whose God is the Lord."

When it was announced that a civil war had commenced between the different States of this Union, the news was every where received with bewildering astonishment. Greater surprise could not have been produced by the announcement of the fulfillment of the apocalyptic vision of "*war in heaven.*" But upon mature deliberation and reflection, we see that there have been causes at work, whose inevitable tendency has been to produce the very state of affairs which we now witness. The United States, after the adoption of the present Constitution, entered upon an era of prosperity entirely unknown in the history of man. In the duration of a single life, our population has increased from three millions to thirty millions, and our wealth has increased in far greater ratio. But amidst all our prosperity, there were those among us who were continually sowing the seeds of discord all over the land, paid for their detestable services with foreign gold. The Constitution was publicly denounced as a "league with death, and a covenant with hell." The ministers of the Gospel who sustained it were declared to be "the ministers of the devil," and their churches "the synagogues of Satan." "SILVER-TONGUED" orators declared that they "would spit upon it, and trample it under their feet." Slavery was declared from the pulpit to be worse than murder, and the slaveholder worse than the murderer. Even the Supreme Court of the nation, which Washington declared to be the key-stone of the Union, has been assailed and denounced by the pulpit and the press. These vile slanders were clearly offenses against the public law of the land, and yet no prosecution followed, for enforcing the penalty of the violated law. When the people allow such language to be used, without attempting to suppress it and punish the offense, it is to be regarded as the general sentiment of the people, and the whole people become responsible for the acts of its individual members. These same men, who have uttered such language from the pulpit, have been sentenced to the penitentiary for less libelous language upon other subjects.

It was quietly whispered in the parlor, that the slave would be justified in murdering his master. Arms were in one case purchased and secretly transferred into slave territory, for the purpose of being placed in the hands of the slaves for that avowed purpose. An arsenal was seized in attempting to produce an insurrection. Innocent men within the range of the arsenal were shot down in the streets, without a moment's warning. The house of a worthy citizen, who bears the name, and in whose veins flows the kindred blood of the "Father of our country," was secretly entered in the night-time, and its occupants dragged from their homes by their felon-captors, and confined for days in such position as to expose their lives to the weapons of their friends, if aimed against their captors. And when a part of these felons found a "felon's doom," they were placed in the calendar of martyrs. On the floor of Congress, the most offensive language has been used, and the slaveholder denounced as the incarnation of all villainies. Retaliation and revenge, on the part of the South, has followed all these offenses. Attempts to tamper with slaves, or to produce insurrection, have been punished with tar, feathers, and hemp. Offensive language uttered in the Senate has been revenged by sprinkling the floor of the Senate Chamber with the blood of the offender.

By such language and such acts, on the part of North and South, one after another of the sacred ties which bound our fathers together as a band of brothers have been severed, Sectional churches, sectional benevolent societies, and sectional political parties, have been formed, and at last, sectional governments are marshaling their hundreds of thousands of armed men to drench the land with fratricidal blood.

As we find ourselves in this unfortunate position, we are bound to look about us, and inquire, if there is any honorable way by which the effusion of blood may be checked, and partial, if not complete, *peace*, *prosperity*, and *happiness*, restored to our bleeding country.

The plan I would propose is as follows:

1. Let a Convention, composed of a number of Delegates equal to the Senators and Representatives in Congress, selected direct from the body of the people, meet in the city of New-York, on Tuesday, the 15th day of October next, to devise some plan for the reconstruction of the Government.

2. Let the question of the division of the United States into two, three, or four Republics, be considered and determined by the Convention.

3. If it shall be determined to divide the United States into two or more Republics, let the question of the union of these and other Republics into a Government, to be known as "The Democratic Empire," be considered and determined by the Convention.

4. If a Union of these Republics shall be agreed upon, let the question of the distribution of the powers of government between the three grades of government, be considered and determined by the Convention.

5. Let the further question of the location of the Capital of the "Democratic Empire," with the formation of a Constitution, be considered and determined by the Convention.

6. Let the conditions of the admission of the "British Provinces in North-America," when they shall become a Republic, together with Mexico and other Republics, into the "Democratic Empire," be considered and determined by the Convention.

7. Let the Convention take into consideration and determine all questions which may arise in the formation of such a Government as will secure to all, domestic tranquillity, peace, prosperity and happiness.

8. Let an Imperial Party be at once organized in every Town, Ward, and District, in the land, to educate and sustain the Empire; and let the people in each Congressional District select one of their most able and judicious citizens to represent them in Convention, to be held in the City of New-York, with full power to proclaim the Empire, prepare a Constitution, and establish a Provisional Imperial Government.

The Constitution I would propose as a basis, subject to the alterations and amendments of the Convention, is as follows:

CONSTITUTION OF THE DEMOCRATIC EMPIRE.

We, the People of the Democratic Empire, fervently supplicating the Almighty Being who presides in the councils of nations, and controls the affairs of men, that his benediction may consecrate our labors to the peace, prosperity, and happiness of our beloved country, do hereby unite and bind ourselves together in a firm and perpetual League of Unity, Amity, Peace, and Commerce; and in order to secure to ourselves and our posterity the blessings of Civil and Religious Liberty, Political Equality, and Perpetual Fraternity, we hereby ordain and establish this Constitution as the supreme and fundamental law of the Empire.

ARTICLE I.

TITLE.

§ 1. This Government shall be known and designated by the title of "The Democratic Empire."

ARTICLE II.

FLAG.

§ 2. The Flag of the Democratic Empire shall be composed of seven colors and thirteen stripes, resembling a double rainbow united, (one to remind us that the earth shall no more be deluged with water; the other, that it shall no more be deluged in blood.) The upper corner, nearest the staff, extending down to the seventh stripe and extending in length five eighths of the flag, shall be blue, upon which shall be placed the two hemispheres united by clasped hands in token of our invitation to all people and nations to come with us and repose beneath its sheltering folds. Upon the blue ground shall be inscribed these four symbolical letters: W. C. P. P.

ARTICLE III.

SEAL.

§ 3. The Seal of the Democratic Empire shall be the figure of a woman standing on the summit of a mountain, with the American Eagle, with half-expanded wings, perched at her feet. She is clothed in a flowing robe of pure gold, bound around the waist with a golden girdle, upon which is inscribed: "Peace over all the earth." "Good-will to all men." On her head is a crown of thirteen stars. Below her, at her right hand, are the summits of many mountains, and the moon is descending among these mountain summits beneath her feet. Above these mountain summits is a cloud. Beneath the cloud the scales of Justice are suspended from a visible hand supported by an arm concealed among the clouds. On one scale is written, "The voice of God," on the other, "The voice of the People." The scales are equally balanced. Upon the beam is inscribed: "Theocratic Democracy." The figure, with her left hand, is pointing towards the cloud. At her right hand are other mountain summits, from among which the morning sun is ascending, throwing its rays upon her golden robes and sparkling crown. Beneath her feet are the dismounted cannon—the broken spear—the sheathed sword. In her right hand are many laurel wreaths. Upon her left arm is inscribed, "Length of Days," and on her right, "Riches and Honor."

ARTICLE IV.

UNITY OF THE EMPIRE.

§ 4. The Empire is one and indivisible, bound together by ten thousand bonds of consanguinity and affinity.

Reciprocal rights and reciprocal duties bind each citizen to the whole Empire, and the whole Empire to each citizen.

ARTICLE V.

POLITICAL EQUALITY.

§ 5. All men, when they form a social compact, are equally under the protection of the law. Their descendants are in many respects created equal and in others totally unequal.

§ 6. They are equally helpless in infancy, equally dependent on the services of others for food and clothing and instruction in childhood, and on account of such helplessness and dependence, subject to the control of others until they arrive to the maturity of manhood.

§ 7. They are totally unequal in their physical and mental constitutions, and in the estates which they inherit from their ancestors. Some inherit from their ancestors a healthy and vigorous constitution, a strong mind, an ample fortune, and trophies of noble deeds descending through a long line of illustrious ancestry. Others inherit from their ancestors a diseased and feeble constitution, a weak and depraved mind, poverty and dishonor, descending through generations of ancestors, so that two persons can hardly be found who are exactly and in all respects alike.

ARTICLE VI.

EDUCATION.

§ 8. A good education in childhood and an opportunity for a constant advancement in the path of progress to successively higher degrees of knowledge, morality and, virtue, is the inalienable right of every citizen of the empire. When he arrives to the maturity of manhood, he is equally bound to contribute to the education and support of the helpless and dependent.

ARTICLE VII.

LABOR.

§ 9. Labor is the source of individual and national wealth. It is the fountain of health, morality, and happiness, and all should be allowed and required to perform some kind of labor.

§ 10. Idleness is the parent of vice and the most prolific source of misery, and no citizen of the Empire should be allowed to lead an idle and dissolute life.

ARTICLE VIII.

RELIGIOUS WORSHIP.

§ 11. The Human Family are the children of one Common Parent, and each has a right to repose in the Father of all, filial. confidence—to regard him with filial affection, and to worship him in such manner as shall be in accordance with the word of God and the dictates of reason and conscience.

§ 12. Every member of the Human Family, actuated by the spirit of concession and compromise, should strive to establish the "unity of the faith" in all the fundamental and essential principles of religious worship, that there may be but "one fold and one shepherd," but civil power should not interfere with or control such worship.

§ 13. The right of conscience should not be extended so far as to protect or authorize any criminal or immoral act, nor should the worship of idols and the sacrifice of human beings as a religious ceremony be anywhere allowed.

ARTICLE IX.

THE OBJECT AND SOURCES OF GOVERNMENT.

§ 14. Governments are instituted among men for the purpose of securing to every citizen the greatest amount of TRUE AND LASTING HAPPINESS. That form of government is best, which will most perfectly secure this object.

§ 15. The most perfect form of government, for the security of the true and lasting happiness of the citizen, is a well-devised and accurately balanced Theocratic Democracy.

§ 16. The Supreme Ruler of the Universe is the Supreme Legislator, and Ruler, and Judge, among the nations.

§ 17. He is the fountain of perfection—the fountain of honor—the giver of preferment. All political power originates with and is derived from him.

§ 18. The fundamental principles upon which governments are formed are coëval with the creation of man, and are anterior and superior to any positive enactment. They are fixed and invariable. They are the supreme constitutional laws of man's existence, to which all legislative enactments must strictly conform. They are defined, but not conferred, by our free Constitutions.

§ 19. To develop and arrange these principles; to reduce them to a written code, under the sanction of legislative enactment; and to carry the same into effect, is the principal object for which governments were instituted, that equal rights and equal privileges may be secured to all.

§ 20. Whenever the course of any government tends to subvert these principles, the people have the right, and it is their imperative duty, to alter, reform, or to change the same entirely, and to substitute therefor such form of government as shall secure to all the highest degree of true and lasting happiness.

ARTICLE X.

OFFICERS OF GOVERNMENT.

§ 21. Although the Supreme Being presides in the councils of nations, and controls the affairs of men, and his will should be consulted and followed in all the affairs of government, yet the Divine will must be carried into effect in human governments through the medium of officers duly selected from the body of the people.

§ 22. The officers of the government are the trustees and servants of the people, to whose keeping, for the time being, the powers of government are confided.

§ 23. The people have the right to demand that the officers of the government be men of high moral and religious character—that those who minister at the sacred altars of justice shall be men of "clean hands and a pure heart"—that when they take the oath of office, and "swear in the presence of the ever-living God, that they will faithfully perform the duties of the office upon which they are about to enter," they may not regard such act as a mere idle ceremony, but as a solemn compact between themselves on the one part, and God and the people on the other, to whom they are accountable for the exercise of the power confided to their keeping. "He that ruleth over men must be just, ruling in the fear of God." The judges "judge not for man, but for the Lord, who is with them in the judgment." "When the righteous are in authority, the people rejoice; but when the wicked bear rule, the people mourn." "Able men, such as fear God—men of truth, hating covetousness," should alone and exclusively be selected as officers of government. The incompetent, the immoral, and the dishonest, should be excluded from the exercise of so sacred a trust.

ARTICLE XI.

SELECTION OF OFFICERS.

§ 24. Every government, through its legislative authority, should describe definitely and minutely, the requisite qualifications for every office in the government, whether it be an office of honor, trust, and profit, or an office of sacrifice, toil, and danger.

§ 25. Every citizen who possesses the requisite qualifications for each office, after thorough examination, should be registered as a candidate for the office for which, on such examination, he has been found to be fully qualified.

§ 26. The selection from the candidates registered to fill every office in the government should be made in the same manner as members of the Grand Inquest are now selected. This was the mode of filling all offices in the most ancient Republics. Precedents of later date are also to be found. By this mode of selection, all political intrigue, all strife for office, and all the consequent evils that follow, will be suppressed. Each citizen who is qualified will be equally liable to be called upon to fill the office for which he is qualified, whether it be an office of honor, trust, and profit, or an office of sacrifice, toil, and danger.

ARTICLE XII.

DEGREES OF GOVERNMENT.

§ 27. There shall be three degrees of government:

1. State government.

2. A Union of State governments into a National government.

3. A Union of National governments into a Democratic Empire.

The boundaries of the American States shall remain as heretofore, subject to such alterations and changes as may be determined by the National government, at the request, or with the consent of the people of the State.

§ 28. The former territory of the United States shall be divided into two national governments. The division line shall be the present boundary between the "Labor States" and the "Capital States," until it reaches the Missouri Compromise line, which line shall be extended west until it reaches the Atlantic Ocean.

§ 29. These two national governments shall be united into a Democratic Empire. The city of New-York shall be the capital of the Democratic Empire. Each National and State government shall determine for itself the locality of its capital.

§ 30. In each degree of government there shall be three branches:

1. Legislative.
2. Judiciary.
3. Executive.

§ 31. It shall be the business of the legislative branch of government to enact such laws as shall tend to the constant advancement of all its citizens to constantly higher grades of education, morality, piety, and happiness, and such as shall tend to the constant decrease of ignorance, immorality, vice, and misery. The Legislature should prohibit and declare unlawful all kinds of traffic and every practice *which tends to crime* and PRODUCES MORE EVIL THAN GOOD TO ITS CITIZENS. The law never speaks but to command; nor commands where it has no power to compel. Consequently there are many *voluntary* duties and undefined offenses which are beyond the power of legislation. Among these are, piety to God; respect of parents; benevolence to the poor; gratitude to benefactors; luxury; prodigality; disrespect to parents; envy, hatred, and malice.

§ 32. It is the certainty of the law that gives stability to a government, and the principles of the common law, which are the accumulated wisdom of ages, should not be overturned and subverted by the Legislature unless enforced by absolute necessity. Hasty and reckless legislation is the bane of any government.

§ 33. The power to make laws may be regarded as the supreme power in the government. It should be placed in the hands of the most able and cautious jurists in the land.

ARTICLE XIII.

THE LEGISLATIVE POWER.

§ 34. The legislative power in each grade of government shall be vested in a Senate and House of Representatives. The members of the State House of Representatives shall be selected annually. Those of the National House of Representatives shall hold their office for two years, and those of the Imperial House of Representatives shall hold their office for four years. The qualifications of Representatives in each degree of government shall be fully and accurately prescribed by the law of the government. No person shall be elegible unless he is fully qualified to fill the office.

§ 35. The members of the State Senate shall hold their office for two years, those of the National Senate for four years, and those of the Imperial Senate for six years. Their number, qualifications, and mode of selection shall be determined by law. Both houses shall be governed by the usual rules of parliamentary proceedings. The legislative body in a State shall be known and designated as a "Legislature;" in a nation as a "Congress;" and in the empire as a "Parliament."

ARTICLE XIV.

JUDICIARY.

§ 36. It shall be the business of the judicial branch of the government, with or without the aid of a jury, to apply the law to every statement of facts duly heard and determined before them. The judicial power shall be vested in courts duly organized by the law of the government.

ARTICLE XV.

EXECUTIVE POWER.

§ 37. The executive power of a State shall be vested in a Governor, who shall hold his office for two years. The executive power of the nation shall be vested in a President, who shall hold his office for four years. The executive power of the empire shall be vested in an Emperor, who shall hold his office for six years. It shall be the business of each to see that the laws of his government are faithfully executed. The Governor, President, and Emperor shall be ineligible for the next succeeding term of office after the term for which he is selected expires. The salary or compensation of each officer of government shall be settled by the law of the government to which he belongs. Every act of the legislative branch of the government shall be presented to the chief executive officer of the government for his signature before it becomes a law. If such executive officer approve the same, he shall sign it; if not, he shall return the same to the branch of the Legislature in which it shall have originated, with his objections thereto. If the same is reconsidered and passed by two thirds of the members of both branches of the Legislature, it shall become a law, notwithstanding the objections of the executive.

ARTICLE XVI.

DISTRIBUTION OF POWERS AMONG THE THREE DEGREES OF GOVERNMENT.

§ 38. The most natural and the most equitable distribution of the powers of government, and that which is most likely to secure permanent peace and good order throughout the empire, should be adopted.

ARTICLE XVII.

POWERS OF THE STATE GOVERNMENT.

§ 39. The State government should have the power to make, apply, and execute all laws peculiar to the State.

§ 40. The people of the State, in their right of sovereignty, possess the original and ultimate title to all the lands within the jurisdiction of the State. The citizen holds his lands subject to the superior title of the people of the State. The people of the State may take such lands or other property *for any public use* upon payment of a just compensation therefor. On failure of title for defect of heirs, the title reverts to the State. Hence the State government should have exclusive authority to make all laws regulating the acquisition, the enjoyment, and the transmission of all the real and personal property within the State.

§ 41. The State regulates the descent of the property of its citizens who die intestate—grants to its citizens power to devise or bequeath their property by last will and testament—defines the right of the widow to dower and the right of the husband to curtesy—defines the powers and duties of executors and administrators—creates corporations—regulates the boundaries of towns, counties, and districts—prescribes the mode of selecting its public officers—organizes its militia for the defense of the State—regulates the assessment and collection of taxes—provides for the public instruction of the children of the State—establishes and regulates highways, bridges, and ferries—provides for the support and maintenance of the poor—provides employment for beggars and vagrants—regulates the navigation of its rivers—prescribes the manner of creating and annulling the marriage contract—defines the effect of such contract upon the property of the parties to the contract—defines the mutual rights and duties of parent and child, guardian and ward, master and servant—establishes or prohibits slavery within its boundaries, and regulates or abolishes the same at pleasure.

§ 42. The State establishes its courts of justice—provides for the protection and enforcement of right, the redress and prevention of wrong—defines the various crimes, and affixes the grade of punishment.

§ 43. These rights, powers, and duties belong exclusively to each and every sovereign State. No other State, and no citizen of another State has a right, under any pretense whatever, to interfere with these domestic rights and institutions.

ARTICLE XVIII.

POWERS OF THE NATIONAL GOVERNMENT.

§ 44. The National Government should have the power to make, apply, and execute all laws which are common to all the States composing the nation.

The National Government must regulate the boundaries of States; control and regulate the national Territories, and provide for their admission as States; control the sale of the national lands; establish courts having jurisdiction of all cases in law and equity, arising under the national Constitution and the national laws; cases which arise between two States of the nation; cases between a State and citizens of another State; cases between citizens of different States.

§ 45. The right of Eminent Domain should exist in the National Government, and the National Government should have the right to take any lands or other property for public use upon paying a just compensation therefor, whenever the safety and welfare of the nation shall require it.

The National Government should make all laws in reference to internal improvements, and control and regulate the post-offices and post-roads within the boundaries of the nation.

ARTICLE XIX.

POWERS OF THE IMPÉRIAL GOVERNMENT.

§ 46. The government of the Democratic Empire should have power to make, apply, and execute all laws which are common to all the Republics comprising the Empire.

§ 47. Among the powers of the Government of the Empire are the following:

1. To hold and control all forts, magazines, arsenals, and navy-yards.
2. To raise and support a standing army.
3. To provide and maintain a navy.
4. To secure domestic tranquillity and provide against foreign invasion.
5. To declare war and conclude treaties of peace.
6. To define and punish felonies committed on the high seas.
7. To establish a uniform tariff for the purposes of revenue, and to regulate the same.
8. To coin money, and regulate the value of foreign coin.
9. To establish a uniform mode of pleading and practice in all courts—State, National, and Imperial.
10. To grant copyrights to authors, and patent-rights to inventors.
11. To establish uniform rules of naturalization.
12. To take such lands or other property as may be necessary for public purposes, upon payment of a just compensation therefor, when the safety and welfare of the nation shall require it.
13. To make all laws necessary for carrying into execution these powers.
14. To establish courts having jurisdiction of all cases in law and equity arising under the Constitution and the Laws of the Empire.

§ 48. When men enter into a state of society they surrender some of their natural rights to that society, in order to insure the protection of others; and whenever that protection ceases, these natural rights at once revert, and the surrender becomes void. There is no allegiance to a government when the government fails or ceases to protect.

ARTICLE XX.

POWER OF THE CITIZEN.

§ 49. When governed by natural law alone, every man has the inherent authority to defend the most insignificant right. In civil society this authority is suspended, because other remedies are provided, and in general he can not take the law into his own hands. But there are natural rights which the individual never surrenders to society. In a state of nature, when an attempt is made to murder a person, or to murder his or her husband or wife, parent or child, master, mistress, or servant, or there is reasonable grounds to apprehend a design to commit a felony upon or to do some great bodily injury to either, and there is eminent danger of its being accomplished, and it becomes necessary to kill the assailant to preserve one's own life, or the life of the family, or to prevent some great bodily injury to either, such killing is justifiable. The case is not altered when he enters into civil society, because the law of society can not interpose to protect him. In all other cases each individual has surrendered the right of self-defense to the society of which he is a member.

§ 50. If a State stands by itself, unconnected with other States, and there is no legal remedy for the protection of rights and the redress of wrongs except by an appeal to arms, that right of self-protection exists in the State. But when that State enters into the society of States it surrenders all the rights of war to the society of States, except in cases of sudden insurrection or invasion, in which the law of the society of States can not immediately interpose to protect the State.

§ 51. So if several Republics enter into a society of Republics, whether called the "Democratic Empire," or distinguished by any other name, it surrenders all the rights of protection by offensive or defensive war to the government of the empire, except in cases of insurrection or invasion, when imminent danger exists, and the power of the Empire can not be immediately interposed.

§ 52. There is in the state of nature a remedy or a penalty for every wrong. He who violates the laws of nature which God has prescribed for the common safety, becomes the enemy of all mankind. The right of government to redress injuries and punish crimes is only the right which every individual originally possessed to execute the laws of nature, and to take care of his own safety.

§ 53. The authority to defend the society of Republics by the power of an army and navy should be exclusively confided to the Imperial Government. War, by this means, will cease forever between State and State, or Republic and Republic, within the Empire. By confining each grade of government to the rights and duties peculiar to that grade, all conflict of jurisdiction will be avoided, and the *foundation laid for a government which may become universal.*

§ 54. Concessions and compromises on the part of all must be the foundation of this compact. The regulation of the domestic institutions of every State must be left to the State, without external interference or reproof or advice. PERFECT *protection of* PERSON *and* PROPERTY *and* CHARACTER *must be guaranteed to all.* Slanderous words, coming from whatever source they may come, must be suppressed and punished. All unkind language, by which the feelings of a fellow-citizen may be injured, should be carefully avoided. Discussions in our legislative halls should be conducted in a spirit of fraternal candor. Each citizen should treat the other with due delicacy and respect. The two belligerent parties should no longer treat each other as enemies. Forgetting the past, harmony and peace should at once be restored. This will be another proof that the manifest destiny of humanity is towards *the union of all men in one indissoluble bond of fraternity.* The sword will then be changed for the plowshare, and the spear for the pruning-hook, and the nations learn war no more.

ARTICLE XXI.

ADMISSION OF OTHER REPUBLICS TO THE DEMOCRATIC EMPIRE.

§ 55. If at any time hereafter, by the consent of Great Britain, the British Provinces in North-America shall be formed into States, and the States united into the Republic of Canada, and such Republic shall, by her constituted authorities, express a wish to become a part of this Democratic Empire, she shall be admitted into the Empire, and be entitled to all the rights and privileges of other Nations of the Empire.

§ 56. If at any time hereafter the Republic of Mexico shall be reörganized by the formation of States, and the union of States into a Republic, after the model of the other States and Republics, and shall, by her constituted authorities, express a wish to become a part of this Democratic Empire, she shall be admitted into the Empire, and be entitled to all the rights and privileges of the other Nations of the Empire.

§ 57. If at any time hereafter the States of Central America and the West-India Islands shall be formed into States, and the States into a Republic, such Republic may be admitted into the Empire, and entitled to all the rights and privileges of the other Nations of the Empire.

§ 58. If South-America shall be organized into States, and the States united into a Republic, such Republic may also be admitted.

By this means the Monroe Doctrine, that the Continent of America should be exclusively under the control of Americans, will be triumphantly vindicated.

ARTICLE XXII.

PUBLIC PROPERTY AND REVENUE.

§ 59. The navies, arsenals, fortifications, navy-yards, custom-houses, mints, ordnance, and all other public property used for the public defense, or for the purposes of collecting the revenue or coining money, shall be under the care and control of the Imperial Government.

§ 60. The Imperial Government shall assume all the national debts of the several Republics when they enter into the Democratic Empire. The Imperial Government shall have the care and control of all the revenue arising from duties levied upon commerce with foreign nations. The revenue thus collected shall be applied, under the direction of the Imperial Government, first, to the expenses of supporting the Imperial Government, with the army and navy, and the balance shall be applied to the extinguishment of the Imperial debt. When such debt shall have been liquidated, the surplus revenue shall be annually distributed to the National Governments in proportion to the amount of taxable property in each Nation. Such surplus shall first be applied to the payment of the expenses of such National Government, and the surplus divided among the several States of the Republic in proportion to the taxable property in each State, to be used for purposes of education or liquidating other expenses of the State.

§ 61. The State Government shall be supported by direct taxation and the internal revenue of the State. The National Government shall be supported by the surplus of the Imperial revenue and the internal revenue of the Nation, arising from the sale of its public lands and other sources, and by direct taxation if other sources shall be insufficient.

§ 62. There shall be free trade throughout the Empire between State and State and between Nation and Nation comprising the Empire.

§ 63. The Emperor shall be Commander-in-chief of the army and navy of the Empire, and of the militia when called into the service of the Empire; but he shall have no power to command in person.

§ 64. The Parliament House and Imperial Palace shall be located on Washington Heights, in the City of New-York.

Done at the City of New-York, in Convention of the American States, by their delegates duly appointed, on Friday, the first day of February, 1861. In witness whereof, we have hereunto subscribed our names.

A—— B——

President and Delegate from

This Constitution, with such alterations and amendments as may be suggested by the accumulated wisdom of the nation in convention assembled, would again place this nation in the sure path of peace, industry, morality, piety, wealth, happiness, glory, dominion, and power.

In conclusion, I would ask if we can not find *something* in history or prophecy to admonish us in this dark hour, as a beacon to warn, or as a star to guide. Read the first eight verses of the sixth chapter of the Revelations.

"And I saw when the Lamb opened one of the seals, and I heard as it were the noise of thunder, one of the four beasts, say, 'Come and see.' And I saw, and behold a *white horse:* and he that sat on him had a bow; and a crown was given unto him: and he went forth conquering and to conquer.

"And when he had opened the second seal, I heard the second beast say, 'Come and see.' And there went out *another horse that was red:* and power was given to him that sat thereon to take peace from the earth, and THAT THEY SHOULD KILL ONE ANOTHER. And there was given unto him a great sword.

"And when he had opened the third seal, I heard the third beast say, 'Come and see.' And I beheld, and lo a black horse; and he that sat on him had a pair of balances in his hand. And I heard a voice from the midst of the four beasts say, 'A measure of wheat for a penny, and three measures of barley for a penny; and see thou hurt not the oil and the wine.'

"And when he had opened the fourth seal, I heard the voice of the fourth beast say, 'Come and see.' And I looked, and behold, a pale horse: and his name that sat on him was Death, and Hell followed with him. And power was given unto them over the fourth part of the earth to kill with sword, and with hunger, and with death, and with the beasts of the earth."

It is believed that this prophecy had its first fulfillment in the rise, progress, decay, and destruction of the Roman Republic. The horse was the national emblem of Rome. The *colors* of the horses indicate the successive stages of conquest, prosperity, adversity, and destruction. The *riders* represent the agents employed to bring about these conditions of the Republic.

The color of the first horse, which was white, indicates the state of prosperity, victory, and expansion of power, which Rome enjoyed for *eighty-three years.* White was the symbol of prosperity, and in triumphal processions the horse was covered with white. During this period Rome was governed by wisdom and virtue, unstained by civil blood, undisturbed by revolution. Our own history finds an exact parallel, and to the same period of time. We have enjoyed our eighty-three years of unequalled prosperity.

The second horse was red, the general and almost universal symbol of blood. "Killing one another" is the language of civil war. The peace they formerly enjoyed was taken from the earth. The pretorian guard, under their chief, during the period of sixty years, assassinated nine Roman emperors in succession. Peace had fled, and a reign of terror foreshadowed the decline and final destruction of Rome.

The third horse was black. Black is the universal symbol of mourning and distress. There followed a condition of extreme poverty and oppression. The black mantle of night hung over the nation. The nation went down rapidly, and soon that stage represented by the Pale Horse.

Death sat upon the horse, and hell followed with him, and power was given to them to kill with the sword, and with hunger, and with death, and with the beasts of the earth. As Rome approached her final dissolution, the sword, pestilence, famine, and even destruction by the beasts of the earth were the dregs of the cup of wrath she was compelled to drink.

We have followed Rome for eighty-five years. Universal prosperity and happiness has been ours. We have abandoned the white horse upon which we went forth from conquering to conquer. We are now on the red horse of civil war, and the temple of liberty is being pulled down over our own heads. How long shall we follow in the footsteps of the once glorious self-destroyed Roman Republic?

STATESMEN AND CITIZENS! The contrast suggests an important lesson.

www.ingramcontent.com/pod-product-compliance
Lightning Source LLC
LaVergne TN
LVHW011136110826
845150LV00008B/2380

* 9 7 8 1 4 1 8 1 9 3 6 1 4 *